The Wonder of Women by John Marston

or, **THE TRAGEDY OF SOPHONISBA**

The Wonder of Women Or The Tragedie of Sophonisba, as it hath beene sundry times Acted at the Blacke Friers.

John Marston was born to John and Maria Marston née Guarsi, and baptised on October 7th, 1576 at Wardington, Oxfordshire.

Marston entered Brasenose College, Oxford in 1592 and earned his BA in 1594. By 1595, he was in London, living in the Middle Temple. His interests were in poetry and play writing, although his father's will of 1599 hopes that he would not further pursue such vanities.

His brief career in literature began with the fashionable genres of erotic epyllion and satire; erotic plays for boy actors to be performed before educated young men and members of the inns of court.

In 1598, he published 'The Metamorphosis of Pigmalion's Image and Certaine Satyres', a book of poetry. He also published 'The Scourge of Villanie', in 1598.

'Histriomastix' regarded as his first play was produced 1599. It's performance kicked off an episode in literary history known as the War of the Theatres; a literary feud between Marston, Jonson and Dekker that lasted until 1602.

However, the playwrights were later reconciled; Marston wrote a prefatory poem for Jonson's 'Sejanus' in 1605 and dedicated 'The Malcontent' to him.

Beyond this episode Marston's career continued to gather both strength, assets and followers. In 1603, he became a shareholder in the Children of Blackfriars company. He wrote and produced two plays with the company. The first was 'The Malcontent' in 1603, his most famous play. His second was 'The Dutch Courtesan', a satire on lust and hypocrisy, in 1604-5.

In 1605, he worked with George Chapman and Ben Jonson on 'Eastward Ho', a satire of popular taste and the vain imaginings of wealth to be found in the colony of Virginia.

Marston took the theatre world by surprise when he gave up writing plays in 1609 at the age of thirty-three. He sold his shares in the company of Blackfriars. His departure from the literary scene may have been because of further offence he gave to the king. The king suspended performances at Blackfriars and had Marston imprisoned.

On 24th September 1609 he was made a deacon and them a priest on 24th December 1609. In October 1616, Marston was assigned the living of Christchurch, Hampshire.

He died (accounts vary) on either the 24th or 25th June 1634 in London and was buried in the Middle Temple Church.

Index of Contents

STORY OF THE PLAY

Syphax and Massinissa, princes of Libya, are rivals for the hand of Sophonisba, daughter of Asdrubal, a powerful Carthaginian nobleman. Massinissa's suit is accepted; whereupon Syphax enters into a league with Scipio, who is advancing against Carthage. On Sophonisba's marriage-night news is brought that the Carthaginian forces stationed at Utica have been defeated by the united armies of Scipio and Syphax. Massinissa is ordered by the senate to march without delay against the enemy; he loyally obeys the command, and takes leave of his virgin-wife. While he is serving Carthage in the field, the Carthaginian senators at home proceed to plot against his life. They determine to gain Syphax to their side by giving him Sophonisba to wife; and Gisco, a physician and skilful empoisoner, is sent to the Carthaginian camp to despatch Massinissa. Among the senators there is an honest old man, Gelosso, who disguises himself, follows Gisco to the camp, and hands Massinissa a letter containing a disclosure of the plot. Massinissa has no sooner dismissed the empoisoner (whom he scorns to punish) than Jugurth, Massinissa's nephew, enters, to announce that Syphax has been seen riding in the direction of Cirta, and that his horsemen are coming at a leisurely pace towards the camp as if to fraternise with

Massinissa's forces. By advice of Gelosso, who lays aside his disguise, Massinissa scatters the horsemen by a sudden onslaught, and hastens to make a league with Scipio. Meanwhile Sophonisba has been sent by the Carthaginian senators to the palace of Syphax at Cirta. She escapes by a subterranean passage that led from the palace to a forest, but through the treachery of her attendant, Zanthia, falls again into the hands of Syphax. In despair of effecting his purpose by persuasion, Syphax applies for help to a powerful enchantress, Erictho, who engages to force Sophonisba by magic to his arms, on condition that he shall speak no word, and have no lights burning, while he embraces her. On the appointed night Syphax discovers to his horror that his embraces have been given to Erictho. While he is cursing his fortunes, a messenger arrives to announce that Scipio and Massinissa are advancing against Cirta. He marches out to meet them; the troops on either side withdraw, while Syphax and Massinissa engage in single combat; Massinissa vanquishes his opponent, but spares his life on receiving assurance that Sophonisba has not suffered outrage. Leaving his prisoner in Scipio's hands, Massinissa hastens to Cirta. He enters the palace with his beaver down, unrecognised by Sophonisba, who throws herself at his feet, and implores him to save her from falling into the hands of the Romans, or grant her instant death. Pledging his oath that he will protect her, he doffs his helmet. The joyful reunion is presently interrupted by the entrance of the Roman general, Lælius, who orders Massinissa to deliver Sophonisba into Scipio's custody (Syphax having represented to Scipio that Sophonisba would quickly induce Massinissa to revolt from Rome). Lælius departs with Massinissa's assurance that the command shall be obeyed. Massinissa is distracted; he must either break the oath that he had pledged to Sophonisba, or he must be faithless in the allegiance that he had sworn to Rome. Sophonisba's heroism rescues him from his dilemma. She declares her willingness to die; he infuses poison in a bowl of wine, and the dauntless woman drinks, speaking words of comfort to her husband as the poison courses through her veins. The lifeless body, laid on a bier, is presented to Scipio by Massinissa.

TO THE GENERAL READER

Know that I have not laboured in this poem to tie myself to relate anything as an historian, but to enlarge everything as a poet. To transcribe authors, quote authorities, and translate Latin prose orations into English blank verse, hath, in this subject, been the least aim of my studies. Then (equal reader) peruse me with no prepared dislike; and, if ought shall displease thee, thank thyself; if ought shall please thee, thank not me: for I confess in this it was not my only end.

ARGUMENTUM

A grateful heart's just height; ingratitude,
And vow's base breach with worthy shame pursued;
A woman's constant love, as firm as fate;
A blameless counsellor well born for state;
The folly to enforce free love: these, know,
This subject with full light doth amply show.

DRAMATIS PERSONÆ

Massinissa, and
Syphax, Kings of Libya, rivals for Sophonisba.
Asdrubal, father to Sophonisba.
Gelosso, a senator of Carthage.
Bytheas, a senator of Carthage.
Hanno Magnus, Captain of Carthage.
Jugurth, Massinissa's nephew.
Scipio, and
Lælius, Generals of Rome.
Vangue, an Æthiopian slave.
Carthalon, a senator of Carthage.
Gisco, a surgeon of Carthage.
Nuntius.
Sophonisba, daughter to Asdrubal of Carthage.
Zanthia, her maid.
Erictho, an enchantress.
Arcathia, and
Nycea, waiting-women to Sophonisba.

SCENE:—Cirta, Carthage, &c.

PROLOGUS

Cornets sounding a march.

Enter at one door the **PROLOGUE**, **TWO PAGES** with torches, **ASDRUBAL** and **JUGURTH**, **TWO PAGES** with lights, **MASSINISSA** leading **SOPHONISBA**, **ZANTHIA** bearing Sophonisba's train, **ARCATHIA** and **NYCEA**, **HANNO** and **BYTHEAS**: at the other door **TWO PAGES** with targets and javelins, **TWO PAGES** with lights, **SYPHAX** arm'd from top to toe, followed by **VANGUE**.

These, thus enter'd, stand still, whilst the Prologue, resting between both troops, speaks.

The scene is Libya, and the subject thus:
Whilst Carthage stood the only awe of Rome,
As most imperial seat of Libya,
Govern'd by statesmen, each as great as kings
(For seventeen kings were Carthage feodars);
Whilst thus she flourish'd, whilst her Hannibal
Made Rome to tremble, and the walls yet pale:
Then in this Carthage Sophonisba lived,
The far-famed daughter of great Asdrubal:
For whom ('mongst others) potent Syphax sues,
And well-graced Massinissa rivals him,
Both princes of proud sceptres: but the lot
Of doubtful favour Massinissa graced,
At which Syphax grows black: for now the night

Yields loud resoundings of the nuptial pomp:
Apollo strikes his harp, Hymen his torch;
Whilst louring Juno, with ill-boding eye,
Sits envious at too forward Venus. Lo,
The instant night: and now ye worthier minds,
To whom we shall present a female glory
(The wonder of a constancy so fix'd,
That fate itself might well grow envious):
Be pleased to sit, such as may merit oil,
And holy dew, still'd from diviner heat.
For rest thus knowing: what of this you hear,
The author lowly hopes, but must not fear:
For just worth never rests on popular frown,
   To have done well is fair deeds' only crown.
Nec se quæsiverit extra.

[Cornets sound a march.

[The **PROLOGUE** leads Massinissa's **TROOPS** over the stage, and departs: Syphax' **TROOPS** only stay.

THE TRAGEDY OF SOPHONISBA

ACT I

SCENE I

The palace of Syphax at Cirta.

SYPHAX and **VANGUE**.

SYPHAX
Syphax, Syphax! why wast thou cursed a king?
What angry god made thee so great, so vile?
Contemn'd, disgracèd! think, wert thou a slave,
Though Sophonisba did reject thy love,
Thy low neglected head, unpointed at,
Thy shame unrumour'd, and thy suit unscoff'd,
Might yet rest quiet. Reputation,
Thou awe of fools and great men; thou that chok'st
Freest addictions, and makest mortals sweat
Blood and cold drops in fear to lose, or hope
To gain, thy never-certain seldom-worthy gracings;
Reputation,
Were't not for thee, Syphax could bear this scorn,
Not spouting up his gall among his blood
In black vexations: Massinissa might

Enjoy the sweets of his preferrèd graces
Without my dangerous envy or revenge;
Were't not for thy affliction, all might sleep
In sweet oblivion: but (O greatness' scourge!)
We cannot without envy keep high name,
Nor yet disgraced can have a quiet shame.

VANGUE
Scipio—

SYPHAX
Some light in depth of hell. Vangue, what hope?

VANGUE
I have received assured intelligence,
That Scipio, Rome's sole hope, hath raised up men,
Drawn troops together for invasion—

SYPHAX
Of this same Carthage?

VANGUE
With this policy,
To force wild Hannibal from Italy—

SYPHAX
And draw the war to Afric?

VANGUE
Right.

SYPHAX
And strike
This secure country with unthought of arms?

VANGUE
My letters bear he is departed Rome,
Directly setting course and sailing up—

SYPHAX
To Carthage, Carthage! O thou eternal youth,
Man of large fame, great and abounding glory,
Renownful Scipio, spread thy two-necked eagles,
Fill full thy sails with a revenging wind,
Strike through obedient Neptune, till thy prows
Dash up our Libyan ooze, and thy just arms
Shine with amazeful terror on these walls!
O now record thy father's honour'd blood

Which Carthage drunk; thy uncle Publius' blood
Which Carthage drunk; thirty thousand souls
Of choice Italians Carthage set on wing:
Remember Hannibal, yet Hannibal,
The consul-queller: O then enlarge thy heart,
Be thousand souls in one! let all the breath,
The spirit of thy name and nation, be mix'd strong
In thy great heart! O fall like thunder-shaft,
The wingèd vengeance of incensèd Jove,
Upon this Carthage! for Syphax here flies off
From all allegiance, from all love or service,
His (now free'd) sceptre once did yield this city.
Ye universal gods, light, heat, and air,
Prove all unblessing Syphax, if his hands
Once rear themselves for Carthage but to curse it!
It had been better they had changed their faith,
Denied their gods, than slighted Syphax' love;
So fearfully will I take vengeance.
I'll interleague with Scipio.—Vangue,
Dear Ethiopian negro, go wing a vessel,
And fly to Scipio: say his confederate,
Vow'd and confirm'd, is Syphax: bid him haste
To mix our palms and arms; will him make up,
Whilst we are in the strength of discontent,
Our unsuspected forces well in arms;
For Sophonisba, Carthage, Asdrubal,
Shall feel their weakness in preferring weakness,
And one less great than we. To our dear wishes,
Haste, gentle negro, that this heap may know
Me and their wrong.

VANGUE
Wrong?

SYPHAX
Ay, tho' 'twere not; yet know, while kings are strong,
What they'll but think, and not what is, is wrong.
I am disgraced in and by that which hath
No reason,—love, and woman; my revenge
Shall therefore bear no argument of right;
Passion is reason when it speaks from might.
I tell thee, man, nor kings nor gods exempt,
But they grow pale if once they find contempt.
Haste!

[Exeunt.

SCENE II

Sophonisba's bedchamber.

Enter **ARCATHIA**; **NYCEA**, with tapers; **SOPHONISBA**, in her night attire, followed by **ZANTHIA**.

SOPHONISBA
Watch at the doors: and till we be reposed
Let no one enter. Zanthia, undo me.

ZANTHIA
With this motto under your girdle:
You had been undone if you had not been undone.
Humblest service!

SOPHONISBA
I wonder, Zanthia, why the custom is,
To use such ceremony, such strict shape,
About us women: forsooth the bride must steal
Before her lord to bed; and then delays,
Long expectations, all against known wishes.
I hate these figures in locution,
These about phases forced by ceremony;
We must still seem to fly what we most seek,
And hide ourselves from what we fain would find.
Let those that think and speak and do just acts,
Know form can give no virtue to their acts,
Nor detract vice.

ZANTHIA
Alas, fair princess! those that are strongly form'd
And truly shap'd, may naked walk; but we,
We things call'd women, only made for show
And pleasure, created to bear children
And play at shuttlecock; we imperfect mixtures,
Without respective ceremony used,
And ever compliment, alas! what are we?
Take from us formal custom and the courtesies
Which civil fashion hath still used to us,
We fall to all contempt. O women, how much,
How much are you beholding to ceremony!

SOPHONISBA
You are familiar. Zanthia, my shoe.

ZANTHIA
'Tis wonder, madam, you tread not awry.

SOPHONISBA
Your reason, Zanthia.

ZANTHIA
You go very high.

SOPHONISBA
Hark! music! music!

[The **LADIES** lay the **PRINCESS** in a fair bed, and close the curtains, whilst **MASSINISSA** Enters.

NYCEA
The bridegroom!

ARCATHIA
The bridegroom!

SOPHONISBA
Haste, good Zanthia: help! keep yet the doors!

ZANTHIA
Fair fall you, lady; so, admit, admit.

[Enter four Boys, anticly attired, with bows and quivers, dancing to the cornets a fantastic measure; **MASSINISSA** in his nightgown, led by **ASDRUBAL** and **HANNO**, followed by **BYTHEAS** and **JUGURTH**. The Boys draw the curtains, discovering **SOPHONISBA**, to whom **MASSINISSA** speaks.

MASSINISSA
You powers of joy, gods of a happy bed,
Show you are pleased; sister and wife of Jove,
High-fronted Juno, and thou Carthage patron,
Smooth-chinn'd Apollo, both give modest heat
And temperate graces!

[**MASSINISSA** draws a white ribbon forth of the bed, as from the waist of **SOPHONISBA**.

Lo, I unloose thy waist!
She that is just in love is god-like chaste.
Io to Hymen!

[**CHORUS**, with cornets, organ and voices. Io to Hymen!

SOPHONISBA
A modest silence, though't be thought
A virgin's beauty and her highest honour;
Though bashful feignings nicely wrought,
Grace her that virtue takes not in, but on her;

What I dare think I boldly speak:
After my word my well-bold action rusheth.
In open flame then passion break!
Where virtue prompts, thought, word, act never blusheth.
Revenging gods, whose marble hands
Crush faithless men with a confounding terror,
Give me no mercy if these bands
I covet not with an unfeignèd fervour;
Which zealous vow when ought can force me t'lame,
Load with that plague Atlas would groan at, shame.
Io to Hymen!

CHORUS
Io to Hymen!

ASDRUBAL
Live both high parents of so happy birth,
Your stems may touch the skies and shadow earth;

Most great in fame, more great in virtue shining.
Prosper, O powers! a just, a strong divining.
Io to Hymen!

CHORUS
Io to Hymen!

[Enter **CARTHALON**, his sword drawn, his body wounded, his shield struck full of darts; **MASSINISSA** being ready for bed.

CARTHALON
To bold hearts Fortune! be not you amazed,
Carthage! O Carthage! be not you amazed.

MASSINISSA
Jove made us not to fear; resolve, speak out;
The highest misery of man is doubt.
Speak, Carthalon!

CARTHALON
The stooping sun, like to some weaker prince,
Let his shades spread to an unnatural hugeness,
When we, the camp that lay at Utica,
From Carthage distant but five easy leagues,
Descried from off the watch three hundred sail,
Upon whose tops the Roman eagles stretch'd
Their large spread wings, which fann'd the evening air,
To us cold breath; for well we might discern
Rome swam to Carthage.

ASDRUBAL

Hannibal, our rancour is come back; thy slight,
Thy stratagem, to lead war unto Rome,
To quite ourselves, hath now taught desperate Rome
T'assail our Carthage: now the war is here.

MASSINISSA

He is nor blest, nor honest, that can fear.

HANNO

Ay, but to cast the worst of our distress—

MASSINISSA

To doubt of what shall be, is wretchedness:
Desire, fear, and hope, receive no bond
By whom, we in ourselves are never but beyond.
On!

CARTHALON

Th' alarum beats necessity of fight;
Th' unsober evening draws out reeling forces,
Soldiers, half men, who to their colours troop
With fury, not with valour: whilst our ships
Unrigg'd, unus'd, fitter for fire than water,
We save in our barr'd haven from surprise.
By this our army marcheth toward the shore,
Undisciplin'd young men, most bold to do,
If they knew how, or what; when we descry
A mighty dust, beat up with horses' hooves:
Straight Roman ensigns glitter; Scipio—

ASDRUBAL

Scipio!

CARTHALON

Scipio, advancèd like the god of blood,
Leads up grim war, that father of foul wounds,
Whose sinewy feet are steep'd in gore, whose hideous voice
Makes turrets tremble and whole cities shake;
Before whose brows flight and disorder hurry;
With whom march burnings, murder, wrong, waste, rapes;
Behind whom a sad train is seen, woe, fears,
Tortures, lean need, famine, and helpless tears.
Now make we equal stand in mutual view:
We judg'd the Romans eighteen thousand foot,
Five thousand horse; we almost doubled them
In number, not in virtue; yet in heat

Of youth and wine, jolly, and full of blood,
We gave the sign of battle: shouts are raised
That shook the heavens; pell-mell our armies join;
Horse, targets, pikes, all against each opposed,
They give fierce shock, arms thunder'd as they clos'd:
Men cover earth, which straight are coverèd
With men and earth; yet doubtful stood the fight,
More fair to Carthage, when lo, as oft we see,
In mines of gold, when labouring slaves delve out
The richest ore, being in sudden hope
With some unlook'd-for vein to fill their buckets,
And send huge treasure up, a sudden damp
Stifles them all, their hands yet stuff'd with gold,—
So fell our fortunes; for look, as we stood proud,
Like hopeful victors, thinking to return
With spoils worth triumph, wrathful Syphax lands
With full ten thousand strong Numidian horse,
And joins to Scipio. Then lo, we all were damp'd;
We fall in clusters, and our wearied troops
Quit all. Slaughter ran through us straight; we fly,
Romans pursue, but Scipio sounds retreat,
As fearing trains and night: we make amain
For Carthage most, and some for Utica,
All for our lives.—New force, fresh arms with speed!

HANNO
You have said truth of all; no more: I bleed.
O wretched fortune!

[Tearing his hair.

MASSINISSA
Old lord, spare thy hairs:
What, dost thou think baldness will cure thy grief?
What decree the Senate?

[Enter **GELOSSO** with commissions in his hand, sealed.

GELOSSO
Ask old Gelosso, who returns from them,
Inform'd with fullest charge. Strong Asdrubal,
Great Massinissa, Carthage general,
So speaks the Senate: counsel for this war
In Hanno Magnus, Bytheas, Carthalon,
And us Gelosso, rests. Embrace this charge,
You never yet dishonour'd Asdrubal,
High Massinissa! by your vows to Carthage,
By th' god of great men,—glory,—fight for Carthage!

Ten thousand strong Massulians, ready troop'd,
Expect their king; double that number waits
The leading of loved Asdrubal: beat loud
Our Afric drums! and, whilst our o'er-toil'd foe
Snores on his unlacked casque, all faint, though proud,
Through his successful fight, strike fresh alarms.
Gods are not if they grace not bold, just arms.

MASSINISSA
Carthage, thou straight shalt know
Thy favours have been done unto a king.

[Exit with **ASDRUBAL** and the **PAGE**.

SOPHONISBA
My lords, 'tis most unusual such sad haps
Of sudden horror should intrude 'mong beds
Of soft and private loves; but strange events
Excuse strange forms. O you that know our blood,
Revenge if I do feign. I here protest,
Though my lord leave his wife a very maid,
Even this night, instead of my soft arms
Clasping his well-strung limbs with glossful steel,
What's safe to Carthage shall be sweet to me.
I must not, nor am I once ignorant
My choice of love hath given this sudden danger
To yet strong Carthage: 'twas I lost the fight;
My choice vex'd Syphax, enraged Syphax struck
Arms' fate; yet Sophonisba not repents:
O we were gods if that we knew events.
But let my lord leave Carthage, quit his virtue,
I will not love him; yet must honour him,
As still good subjects must bad princes. Lords,
From the most ill-graced hymeneal bed
That ever Juno frown'd at, I entreat
That you'll collect from our loose-formèd speech
This firm resolve: that no low appetite
Of my sex' weakness can or shall o'ercome
Due grateful service unto you or virtue.
Witness, ye gods, I never until now
Repined at my creation: now I wish
I were no woman, that my arms might speak
My heart to Carthage. But in vain: my tongue
Swears I am woman still, I talk too long.

[Cornets, a march. Enter **TWO PAGES** with targets and javelins; **TWO PAGES** with torches. **MASSINISSA** armed cap-à-pie; **ASDRUBAL** armed.

MASSINISSA

Ye Carthage lords, know Massinissa knows
Not only terms of honour, but his actions;
Nor must I now enlarge how much my cause
Hath danger'd Carthage, but how I may show
Myself most prest to satisfaction.
The loathsome stain of kings' ingratitude
From me O much be far! And since this torrent,
War's rage, admits no anchor—since the billow
Is risen so high we may not hull, but yield
This ample state to stroke of speedy swords;
What you with sober haste have well decreed,
We'll put to sudden arms; no, not this night,
These dainties, these firstfruits of nuptials,
That well might give excuse for feeble lingerings,
Shall hinder Massinissa. Appetite,
Kisses, loves, dalliance, and what softer joys
The Venus of the pleasing'st ease can minister,
I quit you all. Virtue perforce is vice;
But he that may, yet holds, is manly wise.
Lo then, ye lords of Carthage, to your trust
I leave all Massinissa's treasure: by the oath
Of right good men stand to my fortune just:
Most hard it is for great hearts to mistrust.

CARTHALON

We vow by all high powers.

MASSINISSA

No, do not swear;
I was not born so small to doubt or fear.

SOPHONISBA

Worthy, my lord—

MASSINISSA

Peace, my ears are steel;
I must not hear thy much-enticing voice.

SOPHONISBA

My Massinissa, Sophonisba speaks
Worthy thy wife: go with as high a hand
As worth can rear. I will not stay my lord.
Fight for our country; vent thy youthful heat
In field, not beds: the fruit of honour, Fame,
Be rather gotten than the oft disgrace
Of hapless parents, children. Go, best man,
And make me proud to be a soldier's wife,

That values his renown above faint pleasures:
Think every honour that doth grace thy sword
Trebles my love. By thee I have no lust
But of thy glory. Best lights of heaven with thee!
Like wonder, stand or fall; so, though thou die,
My fortunes may be wretched, but not I.

MASSINISSA
Wondrous creature! even fit for gods, not men:
Nature made all the rest of thy fair sex
As weak essays, to make thee a pattern
Of what can be in woman! Long farewell!
He's sure unconquer'd in whom thou dost dwell,
Carthage Palladium. See that glorious lamp—
Whose lifeful presence giveth sudden flight
To fancies, fogs, fears, sleep, and slothful night—
Spreads day upon the world: march swift amain;—
Fame got with loss of breath is god-like gain!

[The **LADIES** draw the curtains about **SOPHONISBA**; the rest accompany **MASSINISSA** forth: the cornets and organs playing loud full music for the Act.

ACT II

SCENE I

The Senate-house at Carthage.

Whilst the music for the first Act sounds, **HANNO**, **CARTHALON**, **BYTHEAS**, **GELOSSO**, Enter: they place themselves to counsel, **GISCO**, the impoisoner, waiting on them; **HANNO**, **CARTHALON**, and **BYTHEAS** setting their hands to a writing, which being offered to **GELOSSO**, he denies his hand, and, as much offended, impatiently starts up and speaks.

[Enter **GELOSSO**, **HANNO**, **BYTHEAS**, **CARTHALON**.

GELOSSO
My hand? my hand? rot first; wither in aged shame.

HANNO
Will you be so unseasonably wood?

BYTHEAS
Hold such preposterous zeal as stand against
The full decree of Senate, all think fit?

CARTHALON

Nay, most inevitable necessary
For Carthage' safety, and the now sole good
Of present state, that we must break all faith
With Massinissa. Whilst he fights abroad,
Let's gain back Syphax, making him our own,
By giving Sophonisba to his bed.

HANNO
Syphax is Massinissa's greater, and his force
Shall give more side to Carthage: as for's queen,
And her wise father, they love Carthage fate;
Profit and honesty are not one in state.

GELOSSO
And what decrees our very virtuous Senate
Of worthy Massinissa, that now fights,
And (leaving wife and bed) bleeds in good arms
For right old Carthage?

CARTHALON
Thus 'tis thought fit:
Her father, Asdrubal, on sudden shall take in
Revolted Syphax; so with doubled strength,
Before that Massinissa shall suspect,
Slaughter both Massinissa and his troops,
And likewise strike with his deep stratagem
A sudden weakness into Scipio's arms,
By drawing such a limb from the main body
Of his yet powerful army: which being done,
Dead Massinissa's kingdom we decree
To Sophonisba and great Asdrubal
For their consent; so this swift plot shall bring
Two crowns to her, make Asdrubal a king.

GELOSSO
So, first faith's breach, murder, adultery, theft!

CARTHALON
What else?

GELOSSO
Nay, all is done, no mischief left.

CARTHALON
Pish!
Prosperous success gives blackest actions glory;
The means are unremember'd in most story.

GELOSSO
Let me not say gods are not.

CARTHALON
This is fit:
Conquest by blood is not so sweet as wit:
For howsoe'er nice virtue censures it,
He hath the grace of war that hath war's profit.
But Carthage, well advised that states come on
With slow advice, quick execution,
Have here an engineer long bred for plots,
Call'd an impois'ner, who knows this sound excuse:
Th' only dew that makes men sprout in court is use.
Be't well or ill, his thrift is to be mute;
Such slaves must act commands, and not dispute.
Knowing foul deeds with danger do begin,
But with rewards do end: sin is no sin,
But in respects—

GELOSSO
Politic lord, speak low: though Heaven bears
A face far from us, gods have most long ears;
Jove has a hundred marble marble hands.

CARTHALON
O ay, in poetry or tragic scene!

GELOSSO
I fear gods only know what poets mean.

CARTHALON
Yet hear me, I will speak close truth and cease:
Nothing in Nature is unserviceable,
No, not even inutility itself.
Is then for nought dishonesty in being?
And if it be sometimes of forcèd use,
Wherein more urgent than in saving nations?
State shapes are solder'd up with base, nay faulty,
Yet necessary functions: some must lie,
Some must betray, some murder, and some all;
Each hath strong use, as poison in all purges:
Yet when some violent chance shall force a state
To break given faith, or plot some stratagems,
Princes ascribe that vile necessity
Unto Heaven's wrath. And sure, though't be no vice,
Yet 'tis bad chance: states must not stick too nice,
For Massinissa's death sense bids forgive:
Beware t'offend great men, and let them live;

For 'tis of empire's body the main arm,—
He that will do no good shall do no harm.
You have my mind.

GELOSSO
Although a stage-like passion, and weak heat,
Full of an empty wording, might suit age,
Know I'll speak strongly truth. Lords, ne'er mistrust,
That he who'll not betray a private man
For his country, will ne'er betray his country
For private men; then give Gelosso faith.
If treachery in state be serviceable,
Let hangmen do it. I am bound to lose
My life, but not mine honour, for my country.
Our vows, our faith, our oaths, why they're ourselves,
And he that's faithless to his proper self
May be excus'd if he break faith with princes.
The gods assist just hearts, and states that trust
Plots before Providence are toss'd like dust.
For Massinissa (O, let me slack a little
Austere discourse and feel humanity!)
Methinks I hear him cry, "O fight for Carthage!
Charge home! wounds smart not for that so just, so great,
So good a city." Methinks I see him yet
Leave his fair bride, even on his nuptial night,
To buckle on his arms for Carthage. Hark!
Yet, yet, I hear him cry,—"Ingratitude,
Vile stain of man, O ever be most far
From Massinissa's breast! Up, march amain;
Fame got by loss of breath is god-like gain!"
And see, by this he bleeds in doubtful fight,
And cries "For Carthage!" whilst Carthage—Memory,
Forsake Gelosso! would I could not think,
Nor hear, nor be, when Carthage is
So infinitely vile! See, see! look here!

[Cornets. Enter **TWO USHERS**; **SOPHONISBA**, **ZANTHIA**, and **ARCATHIA**; **HANNO**, **BYTHEAS**, and
CARTHALON present **SOPHONISBA** with a paper, which she having perused, after a short silence,
speaks.

SOPHONISBA
Who speaks? What, mute? Fair plot! What? blush to break it?
How lewd to act when so shamed but to speak it.
Is this the Senate's firm decree?

CARTHALON
It is.

SOPHONISBA
Is this the Senate's firm decree?

CARTHALON
It is.

SOPHONISBA
Hath Syphax entertained the stratagem?

CARTHALON
No doubt he hath or will.

SOPHONISBA
My answer's thus,
What's safe to Carthage shall be sweet to us.

CARTHALON
Right worthy.

HANNO
Royalest.

GELOSSO
O very woman!

SOPHONISBA
But 'tis not safe for Carthage to destroy.
Be most unjust, cunningly politic,
Your head's still under heaven. O trust to Fate:
Gods prosper more a just than crafty state;
'Tis less disgrace to have a pitied loss,
Than shameful victory.

GELOSSO
O very angel!

SOPHONISBA
We all have sworn good Massinissa faith;
Speech makes us men, and there's no other bond
'Twixt man and man but words. O equal gods!
Make us once know the consequence of vows—

GELOSSO
And we shall hate faith-breakers worse than man-eaters.

SOPHONISBA
Ha, good Gelosso, is thy breath not here?

GELOSSO

You do me wrong: as long as I can die,
Doubt you that old Gelosso can be vile?
States may afflict, tax, torture, but our minds
Are only sworn to Jove. I grieve, and yet am proud
That I alone am honest: high powers, ye know
Virtue is seldom seen with troops to go.

SOPHONISBA

Excellent man! Carthage and Rome shall fall
Before thy fame.—Our lords, know I the worst?

CARTHALON

The gods foresaw, 'tis fate we thus are forc'd.

SOPHONISBA

Gods naught foresee, but see, for to their eyes
Naught is to come or past; nor are you vile
Because the gods foresee; for gods, not we,
See as things are; things are not as we see.
But since affected wisdom in us women
Is our sex' highest folly, I am silent;
I cannot speak less well, unless I were
More void of goodness. Lords of Carthage, thus:
The air and earth of Carthage owes my body;
It is their servant; what decree they of it?

CARTHALON

That you remove to Cirta, to the palace
Of well-form'd Syphax, who with longing eyes
Meets you: he that gives way to Fate is wise.

SOPHONISBA

I go: what power can make me wretched? what evil
Is there in life to him that knows life's loss
To be no evil? show, show thy ugliest brow,
O most black chance; make me a wretched story:
Without misfortune virtue hath no glory;
Opposèd trees makes tempests show their power,
And waves forced back by rocks makes Neptune tower,—
Tearless O see a miracle of life,
A maid, a widow, yet a hapless wife!

[Cornets. **SOPHONISBA**, accompanied with the **SENATORS**, departs; only **GELOSSO** stays.

GELOSSO

A prodigy! let Nature run cross-legg'd,
Ops go upon his head, let Neptune burn,

Cold Saturn crack with heat, for now the world
Hath seen a woman!
Leap nimble lightning from Jove's ample shield,
And make at length an end! The proud hot breath
Of thee-contemning greatness; the huge drought
Of sole self-loving vast ambition;
Th' unnatural scorching heat of all those lamps
Thou rear'dst to yield a temperate fruitful heat;
Relentless rage, whose heart hath no one drop
Of human pity;—all, all loudly cry,
Thy brand, O Jove, for now the world is dry!
O let a general end save Carthage fame!
When worlds do burn, unseen's a city's flame.
Phœbus in me is great; Carthage must fall;
Jove hates all vice, but vows' breach worst of all.

[Exit.

SCENE II

Near Cirta.

Cornets sound a charge. Enter **MASSINISSA** in his gorget and shirt, shield, sword; his arm transfix'd with a dart. **JUGURTH** follows, with his cuirass and casque.

MASSINISSA
Mount us again; give us another horse!

JUGURTH
Uncle, your blood flows fast: pray ye withdraw.

MASSINISSA
O Jugurth, I cannot bleed too fast, too much,
For that so great, so just, so royal Carthage!
My wound smarts not, blood's loss makes me not faint,
For that loved city. O nephew, let me tell thee,
How good that Carthage is: it nourish'd me,
And when full time gave me fit strength for love,
The most adorèd creature of the city,
To us before great Syphax did they yield,—
Fair, noble, modest, and 'bove all, my own,
My Sophonisba! O Jugurth, my strength doubles:
I know not how to turn a coward,—drop
In feeble baseness I cannot. Give me horse!
Know I'm Carthage' very creature, and am grac'd
That I may bleed for them. Give me fresh horse!

JUGURTH

He that doth public good for multitude,
Finds few are truly grateful.

MASSINISSA

O Jugurth! fie! you must not say so. Jugurth,
Some common-weals may let a noble heart
Even bleed to death abroad, and not bemoan'd,
Neither revenged, at home. But, Carthage, fie!
It cannot be ungrate, faithless through fear:
It cannot, Jugurth: Sophonisba's there.
Beat a fresh charge!

[Enter **ASDRUBAL**, his sword drawn, reading a letter; **GISCO** follows him.

ASDRUBAL

Sound the retreat; respect your health, brave prince;
The waste of blood throws paleness on your face.

MASSINISSA

By light, my heart's not pale: O my loved father,
We bleed for Carthage; balsam to my wounds,
We bleed for Carthage; shall's restore the fight?
My squadron of Massulians yet stands firm.

ASDRUBAL

The day looks off from Carthage; cease alarms!
A modest temperance is the life of arms.
Take our best surgeon Gisco; he is sent
From Carthage to attend your chance of war.

GISCO

We promise sudden ease.

MASSINISSA

Thy comfort's good.

ASDRUBAL

—That nothing can secure us but thy blood!
Infuse it in his wound, 'twill work amain.

GISCO

—O Jove!

ASDRUBAL

—What Jove? thy god must be thy gain,—
And as for me—Apollo Pythian,

Thou know'st a statist must not be a man.

[Exit **ASDRUBAL**.

Enter **GELOSSO** disguised like an old soldier, delivering to **MASSINISSA** (as he is preparing to be dressed by **GISCO**) a letter, which **MASSINISSA** reading, starts, and speaks to **GISCO**.

MASSINISSA
Forbear; how art thou call'd?

GISCO
Gisco, my lord.

MASSINISSA
Um, Gisco. Ha! touch not my arm.—
[To **GELOSSO**]
Most only man!—
[To **GISCO**]
Sirra, sirra, art poor?

GISCO
Not poor.

MASSINISSA
Nephew, command

[**MASSINISSA** begins to draw.

Our troops of horse make indisgraced retreat;
Trot easy off.—Not poor!—Jugurth, give charge
My soldiers stand in square battalia,

[Exit **JUGURTH**.

Entirely of themselves.—Gisco, th' art old;
'Tis time to leave off murder; thy faint breath
Scarce heaves thy ribs, thy gummy blood-shut eyes
Are sunk a great way in thee, thy lank skin
Slides from thy fleshless veins: be good to men.
Judge him, ye gods: I had not life to kill
So base a creature. Hold, Gisco, live;
The god-like part of kings is to forgive.

GISCO
Command astonish'd Gisco.

MASSINISSA
No, return.

Haste unto Carthage, quit thy abject fears,
Massinissa knows no use of murderers.

[Exit **GISCO**.

[Enter **JUGURTH**, amazed, his sword drawn.

Speak, speak! let terror strike slaves mute,
Much danger makes great hearts most resolute.

JUGURTH
Uncle, I fear foul arms; myself beheld
Syphax on high speed run his well-breath'd horse
Direct to Cirta, that most beauteous city
Of all his kingdom; whilst his troops of horse,
With careless trot, pace gently toward our camp,
As friends to Carthage. Stand on guard, dear uncle;
For Asdrubal, with yet his well-rank'd army,
Bends a deep threat'ning brow to us, as if
He waited but to join with Syphax' horse,
And hew us all to pieces. O my king,
My uncle, father, captain, O over all!
Stand like thyself, or like thyself now fall!
Thy troops yet hold good ground. Unworthy wounds,
Betray not Massinissa!

MASSINISSA
Jugurth, pluck,
Pluck! so, good coz.

JUGURTH
O God! Do you not feel?

MASSINISSA
Not, Jugurth, no; now all my flesh is steel.

GELOSSO
Off base disguise! high lights scorn not to view
A true old man. Up, Massinissa! throw
The lot of battle upon Syphax' troops,
Before he join with Carthage; then amain
Make through to Scipio; he yields safe abodes:
Spare treachery, and strike the very gods.

MASSINISSA
Why wast thou born at Carthage! O my fate!
Divinest Sophonisba! I am full
Of much complaint, and many passions,

The least of which express'd would sad the gods,
And strike compassion in most ruthless hell.
Up, unmaim'd heart, spend all thy grief and rage
Upon thy foe! the field's a soldier's stage,
On which his action shows. If you are just,
And hate those that contemn you, O you gods,
Revenge worthy your anger, your anger! O,
Down man, up heart! stoop Jove, and bend thy chin
To thy large breast; give sign th'art pleased, and just;
Swear good men's foreheads must not print the dust.

[Exeunt.

SCENE III

Carthage.

Enter **ASDRUBAL**, **HANNO**, **BYTHEAS**.

ASDRUBAL
What Carthage hath decreed, Hanno, is done;
Advanced and born was Asdrubal for state;
Only with it, his faith, his love, his hate,
Are of one piece. Were it my daughter's life
That, fate hath sung, to Carthage safety brings,
What deed so red but hath been done by kings?
Iphigenia—He that's a man for men,
Ambitious as a god, must, like a god,
Live free from passions; his full aim'd at end,
Immense to others, sole self to comprehend,
Round in's own globe; not to be clasp'd, but holds
Within him all; his heart being of more folds
Than shield of Telamon, not to be pierc'd, though struck:
The god of wise men is themselves, not luck.

[Enter **GISCO**.

See him by whom now Massinissa is not.
Gisco, is't done?

GISCO
Your pardon, worthy lord,
It is not done, my heart sunk in my breast,
His virtue mazed me, faintness seized me all:
Some god's in kings, that will not let them fall.

ASDRUBAL

His virtue mazed thee! (umh) why now I see
Th'art that just man that hath true touch of blood,
Of pity, and soft piety. Forgive?
Yes, honour thee; we did it but to try
What sense thou hadst of blood. Go, Bytheas,
Take him into our private treasury—
[Aside to **BYTHEAS**]
And cut his throat; the slave hath all betray'd.

BYTHEAS

—Are you assured?

ASDRUBAL

—Afear'd, for this I know,
Who thinketh to buy villainy with gold,
Shall ever find such faith so bought, so sold.—
Reward him thoroughly.

[A shout; the cornets giving a flourish.

HANNO

What means this shout?

ASDRUBAL

Hanno, 'tis done. Syphax' revolt by this
Hath secured Carthage; and now his force come in,
And join'd with us, give Massinissa charge,
And assured slaughter. O ye powers! forgive,
Through rotten'st dung best plants both sprout and live;
By blood vines grow.

HANNO

But yet think, Asdrubal,
'Tis fit at least you bear grief's outward show;
It is your kinsman bleeds. What need men know
Your hand is in his wounds? 'Tis well in state
To do close ill, but 'void a public hate.

ASDRUBAL

Tush, Hanno! let me prosper, let routs prate;
My power shall force their silence or my hate.
I scorn their idle malice: men of weight
Know, he that fears envy let him cease to reign;
The people's hate to some hath been their gain.
For howsoe'er a monarch feigns his parts,
Steal anything from kings but subjects' hearts.

[Enter **CARTHALON** leading in bound **GELOSSO**.

CARTHALON
Guard, guard the camp!—make to the trench!—stand firm!

ASDRUBAL
The gods of boldness with us!—how runs chance?

CARTHALON
Think, think how wretched thou canst be, thou art;
Short words shall speak long woes.

GELOSSO
Mark, Asdrubal.

CARTHALON
Our bloody plot to Massinissa's ear
Untimely by this lord was all betrayed.

GELOSSO
By me it was; by me, vile Asdrubal;
I joy to speak't.

ASDRUBAL
Down, slave!

GELOSSO
I cannot fall.

CARTHALON
Our train's disclosed, straight to his well-used arms
He took himself, rose up with all his force
On Syphax' careless troops, Syphax being hurried
Before to Cirta, fearless of success,
Impatient Sophonisba to enjoy;
Gelosso rides to head of all our squadrons,
Commands make stand in thy name, Asdrubal,
In mine, in his, in all: they all obey;
Whilst Massinissa, now with more than fury,
Chargeth the loose and much-amazèd ranks
Of absent Syphax, who with broken shout
(In vain expecting Carthage secondings)
Give faint repulse. A second charge is given:
Then look, as when a falcon towers aloft,
Whole shoals of fowl and flocks of lesser birds
Crouch fearfully, and dive; some among sedge,
Some creep in brakes: so Massinissa's sword,
Brandish'd aloft, toss'd 'bout his shining casque,

Made stoop whole squadrons; quick as thought he strikes,
Here hurls he darts, and there his rage-strong arm
Fights foot to foot; here cries he "strike! they sink!"
And then grim slaughter follows; for by this,
As men betray'd, they curse us, die, or fly, or both;
Six thousand fell at once. Now was I come,
And straight perceived all bled by his vile plot.

GELOSSO
Vile! Good plot! my good plot, Asdrubal!

CARTHALON
I forced our army beat a running march;
But Massinissa struck his spurs apace
Upon his speedy horse, leaves slaughtering;
All fly to Scipio, who with open ranks
In view receives them: all I could effect
Was but to gain him.

ASDRUBAL
Die!

GELOSSO
Do what thou can,
Thou canst but kill a weak old honest man.

[**GELOSSO** departs, guarded.

CARTHALON
Scipio and Massinissa by this strike
Their claspèd palms, then vow an endless love;
Straight a joint shout they raise, then turn they breasts
Direct on us, march strongly toward our camp,
As if they dared us fight. O Asdrubal,
I fear they'll force our camp.

ASDRUBAL
Break up and fly.—
This was your plot.

HANNO
But 'twas thy shame to choose it.

CARTHALON
He that forbids not offence, he does it.

ASDRUBAL
The curse of women's words go with you.—Fly!—

You are no villains!—Gods and men, which way?—
Advise vile things!

HANNO
Vile?

ASDRUBAL
Ay!

CARTHALON
Not?

BYTHEAS
You did all.

ASDRUBAL
Did you not plot?

CARTHALON
Yielded not Asdrubal?

ASDRUBAL
But you enticed me.

HANNO
How?

ASDRUBAL
With hope of place.

CARTHALON
He that for wealth leaves faith, is abject.

HANNO
Base.

ASDRUBAL
Do not provoke my sword; I live.

CARTHALON
More shame,
T' outlive thy virtue and thy once great name.

ASDRUBAL
Upbraid ye me?

HANNO
Hold!

CARTHALON
Know that only thou
Art treacherous: thou shouldst have had a crown.

HANNO
Thou didst all, all; he for whom mischief's done,
He does it.

ASDRUBAL
Brook open scorn, faint powers!—
Make good the camp!—No, fly!—yes, what?—wild rage!—
To be a prosperous villain! yet some heat, some hold;
But to burn temples, and yet freeze, O cold!
Give me some health; now your blood sinks: thus deeds
Ill nourish'd rot; without Jove nought succeeds.

[Exeunt.

ACT III

SCENE I

The Palace of Syphax at Cirta.

SYPHAX, with his dagger twon about her hair, drags in **SOPHONISBA** in her nightgown and petticoat; **ZANTHIA** and **VANGUE** following.

SYPHAX
Must we entreat? sue to such squeamish ears?
Know, Syphax has no knees, his eyes no tears;
Enragèd love is senseless of remorse.
Thou shalt, thou must: kings' glory is their force.
Thou art in Cirta, in my palace, fool:
Dost think he pitieth tears that knows to rule?
For all thy scornful eyes, thy proud disdain,
And late contempt of us, now we'll revenge,
Break stubborn silence. Look, I'll tack thy head
To the low earth, whilst strength of two black knaves
Thy limbs all wide shall strain. Prayer fitteth slaves,
Our courtship be our force: rest calm as sleep,
Else at this quake; hark, hark, we cannot weep.

SOPHONISBA
Can Sophonisba be enforc'd?

SYPHAX
Can? see.

SOPHONISBA
Thou mayest enforce my body, but not me.

SYPHAX
Not?

SOPHONISBA
No.

SYPHAX
No?

SOPHONISBA
No: off with thy loathèd arms,
That lie more heavy on me than the chains
That wear deep wrinkles in the captive's limbs!
I do beseech thee.

SYPHAX
What?

SOPHONISBA
Be but a beast,
Be but a beast.

SYPHAX
Do not offend a power
Can make thee more than wretched: yield to him
To whom fate yields. Know, Massinissa's dead.

SOPHONISBA
Dead!

SYPHAX
Dead.

SOPHONISBA
To gods' and good men's shame.

SYPHAX
Help, Vangue, my strong blood boils.

SOPHONISBA
O yet save thine own fame.

SYPHAX

All appetite is deaf; I will, I must.
Achilles' armour could not bar out lust.

SOPHONISBA

Hold thy strong arm, and hear me. Syphax, know
I am thy servant now: I needs must love thee,
For (O, my sex, forgive!) I must confess
We not affect protesting feebleness,
Entreats, faint blushings, timorous modesty;
We think our lover is but little man,
Who is so full of woman. Know, fair Prince,
Love's strongest arm's not rude; for we still prove,
Without some fury there's no ardent love.
We love our love's impatience of delay;
Our noble sex was only born t'obey,
To him that dares command.

SYPHAX

Why, this is well;
Th' excuse is good: wipe thy fair eyes, our Queen,
Make proud thy head; now feel more friendly strength
Of thy lord's arm: come, touch my rougher skin
With thy soft lip. Zanthia, dress our bed.
Forget old loves, and clip him that through blood
And hell acquires his wish; think not but kiss,
The flourish fore love's fight and Venus' bliss.

SOPHONISBA

Great dreadful lord, by thy affection,
Grant me one boon. Know I have made a vow—

SYPHAX

Vow! what vow? speak.

SOPHONISBA

Nay, if you take offence,
Let my soul suffer first, and yet—

SYPHAX

Offence?
Not, Sophonisba; hold, thy vow is free
As—come, thy lips!

SOPHONISBA

Alas, cross misery!
As I do wish to live, I long t'enjoy
Your warm embrace; but, oh my vow, 'tis thus:

If ever my lord died, I vow'd to him
A most, most private sacrifice, before
I touch'd a second spouse. All I implore,
Is but this liberty.

SYPHAX
This? go, obtain.
What time?

SOPHONISBA
One hour.

SYPHAX
Sweet, good speed, speed, adieu!—
Yet, Syphax, trust no more than thou may'st view.—
Vangue shall stay.

SOPHONISBA
He stays.

[Enter a **PAGE**, delivering a letter to **SOPHONISBA**, which she privately reads.

SYPHAX
Zanthia, Zanthia!
Thou art not foul, go to; some lords are oft
So much in love with their known ladies' bodies,
That they oft love their—Vails: hold, hold, thou'st find
To faithful care kings' bounty hath no shore.

ZANTHIA
You may do much.

SYPHAX
But let my gold do more.

ZANTHIA
I am your creature.

SYPHAX
Be yet; 'tis no stain;
The god of service is however gain.

[Exit.

SOPHONISBA
Zanthia, where are we now? speak worth my service;
Ha' we done well?

ZANTHIA

Nay, in height of best
I fear'd a superstitious virtue would spoil all,
But now I find you above women rare.
She that can time her goodness hath true care
Of her best good. Nature at home begins;
She, whose integrity herself hurts, sins.
For Massinissa, he was good, and so;
But he is dead, or worse, distress'd, or more
Than dead, or much distress'd. O sad, poor,—
Who ever held such friends? no, let him go;
Such faith is praised, then laugh'd at; for still know
Those are the living women that reduce
All that they touch unto their ease and use,
Knowing that wedlock, virtue, or good names,
Are courses and varieties of reason,
To use or leave, as they advantage them,
And absolute within themselves reposed,
Only to greatness ope, to all else closed.
Weak sanguine fools are to their own good nice;
Before I held you virtuous, but now wise.

SOPHONISBA

Zanthia, victorious Massinissa lives,
My Massinissa lives. O steady powers,
Keep him as safe as heaven keeps the earth,
Which looks upon it with a thousand eyes!
That honest valiant man! and Zanthia,
Do but record the justice of his love,
And my for ever vows, for ever vows!

ZANTHIA

Ay, true madam; nay, think of his great mind,
His most just heart, his all of excellence,
And such a virtue as the gods might envy.
Against this, Syphax, is but—and you know,
Fame lost, what can be got that's good for—

SOPHONISBA

Hence!
Take, nay, with one hand.

ZANTHIA

My service.

SOPHONISBA

Prepare
Our sacrifice.

ZANTHIA
But yield you, ay or no?

SOPHONISBA
When thou dost know.

ZANTHIA
What then?

SOPHONISBA
Then thou wilt know.

[Exit **ZANTHIA**.

Let him that would have counsel 'void th' advice
Of friends, made his with weighty benefits,
Whose much dependence only strives to fit
Humour, not reason, and so still devise
In any thought to make their friend seem wise.
But above all, O fear a servant's tongue,
Like such as only for their gain do serve.
Within the vast capacity of space,
I know no vileness so most truly base.
Their lord's their gain; and he that most will give,
With him (they will not die, but) they will live.
Traitors and these are one; such slaves once trust,
Whet swords to make thine own blood lick the dust.

[Cornets and organs playing full music, enter under the conduct of **ZANTHIA** and **VANGUE**, the solemnity of a sacrifice; which being entered, whilst the **ATTENDANTS** furnish the altar, **SOPHONISBA** sings a song; which done, she speaks.

Withdraw, withdraw; all but Zanthia and Vangue depart.—

[Exeunt **ATTENDANTS**.

I not invoke thy arm, thou god of sound,—
Nor thine, nor thine,—although in all abound
High powers immense. But jovial Mercury,
And thou, O brightest female of the sky,
Thrice-modest Phœbe, you that jointly fit
A worthy chastity and a most chaste wit,
To you corruptless honey and pure dew
Upbreathes our holy fire; words just and few,
O deign to hear! if in poor wretches' cries
You glory not; if drops of withered eyes
Be not your sport, be just; all that I crave

Is but chaste life, or an untainted grave.
I can no more; yet hath my constant tongue
Let fall no weakness, tho' my heart were wrung
With pangs worth hell; whilst great thoughts stop our tears,
Sorrow unseen, unpitied, inward wears:
You see now where I rest, come is my end.
Cannot Heaven virtue 'gainst weak chance defend?
When weakness hath out-borne what weakness can,—
What should I say?—'tis Jove's, not sin of man.
—Some stratagem now! let wit's God be shown,
Celestial powers by miracles are known.
I have't; 'tis done.—Zanthia, prepare our bed.
Vangue!

VANGUE
Your servant.

SOPHONISBA
Vangue, we have perform'd
Due rites unto the dead.

[**SOPHONISBA** presents a carouse to **VANGUE**.

Now to thy lord, great Syphax, healthful cups,
Which done, the king is right much welcome.

VANGUE
Were it as deep as thought, off it should thus.

[He drinks.

SOPHONISBA
My safety with that draught.

VANGUE
Close the vault's mouth lest we do slip in drink.

SOPHONISBA
To what use, gentle negro, serves this cave,
Whose mouth thus opens so familiarly,
Even in the king's bedchamber?

VANGUE
O, my queen,
This vault with hideous darkness, and much length,
Stretcheth beneath the earth into a grove,
One league from Cirta (I am very sleepy);
Through this, when Cirta hath been strong begirt,

With hostile siege the king hath safely 'scaped
To, to—

SOPHONISBA
The wine is strong.

VANGUE
Strong?

SOPHONISBA
Zanthia!

ZANTHIA
What means my princess?

SOPHONISBA
Zanthia, rest firm
And silent. Help us; nay, do not dare refuse.

ZANTHIA
The negro's dead!

SOPHONISBA
No, drunk.

ZANTHIA
Alas!

SOPHONISBA
Too late!
Her hand is fearful whose mind's desperate.
It is but sleepy opium he hath drunk.
Help, Zanthia!

[They lay **VANGUE** in Syphax' bed and draw the curtains.

There lie Syphax' bride; a naked man is soon undress'd;
There bide dishonoured passion.

[They knock within, forthwith **SYPHAX** comes.

SYPHAX
Way for the king!

SOPHONISBA
Straight for the king. I fly
Where misery shall see nought but itself.
Dear Zanthia, close the vault when I am sunk,

And whilst he slips to bed, escape; be true;
I can no more; come to me. Hark, gods, my breath
Scorns to crave life, grant but a well-famed death.

[She descends.

[Enter **SYPHAX**, ready for bed, with **ATTENDANTS**.

SYPHAX
Each man withdraw, let not a creature stay
Within large distance.

ZANTHIA
Sir!

SYPHAX
Hence, Zanthia!
Not thou shalt hear; all stand without ear-reach
Of the soft cries nice shrinking brides do yield,
When—

ZANTHIA
But, sir—

SYPHAX
Hence!—stay, take thy delight by steps,
Think of thy joys, and make long thy pleasures.
O silence, thou dost swallow pleasure right;
Words take away some sense from our delight.
Music!
Be proud, my Venus; Mercury, thy tongue;
Cupid, thy flame; 'bove all, O Hercules,
Let not thy back be wanting; for now I leap
To catch the fruit none but the gods should reap.

[Offering to leap into bed, he discovers **VANGUE**.

Hah! can any woman turn to such a devil?
Or—or—Vangue, Vangue—

VANGUE
Yes, yes.

SYPHAX
Speak, slave!
How camest thou here?

VANGUE

Here?

SYPHAX
Zanthia, Zanthia!
Where's Sophonisba? speak at full—at full.
Give me particular faith, or know thou art not—

ZANTHIA
Your pardon, just-moved prince, and private ear.

SYPHAX
Ill actions have some grace, that they can fear.

VANGUE
How came I laid? which way was I made drunk?
Where am I? think I, or is my state advanced?
O Jove, how pleasant is it but to sleep,
In a king's bed!

SYPHAX
Sleep there thy lasting sleep,
Improvident, base, o'er-thirsty slave.

[**SYPHAX** kills **VANGUE**.

Die pleased, a king's couch is thy too-proud grave.—
Through this vault say'st thou?

ZANTHIA
As you give me grace
To live, 'tis true.

SYPHAX
We will be good to Zanthia;
Go, cheer thy lady, and be private to us.

ZANTHIA
As to my life.

[She descends after **SOPHONISBA**.

SYPHAX
I'll use this Zanthia,
And trust her as our dogs drink dangerous Nile
(Only for thirst), that fly the crocodile.
Wise Sophonisba knows love's tricks of art:
Without much hindrance pleasure hath no heart.
Despite all virtue or weak plots I must:

Seven-wallèd Babel cannot bar out lust.

[Descends through the vault.

Neighbourhood of Utica.

Enter **SCIPIO** and **LÆLIUS,** with the complements of Roman **GENERALS** before them. At the other door, **MASSINISSA** and **JUGURTH.** Cornets sound marches.

MASSINISSA
Let not the virtue of the world suspect
Sad Massinissa's faith; nor once condemn
Our just revolt. Carthage first gave me life;
Her ground gave food, her air first lent me breath:
The earth was made for men, not men for earth.
Scipio, I do not thank the gods for life,
Much less vile men, or earth; know, best of lords,
It is a happy being, breath well famed,
For which Jove sees these thus. Men, be not fool'd
With piety to place, tradition's fear;
A just man's country Jove makes everywhere.

SCIPIO
Well urgeth Massinissa; but to leave
A city so ingrate, so faithless, so more vile
Than civil speech can name, fear not; such vice
To scourge is Heaven's grateful sacrifice.
Thus all confess, first they have broke a faith
To thee most due, so just to be observed,
That barbarousness itself may well blush at them:
Where is thy passion? They have shared thy crown,
The proper right of birth, contrived thy death:
Where is thy passion? Given thy beauteous spouse
To thy most hated rival. Statue, not man!
And last, thy friend Gelosso (man worth gods)
With tortures have they rent to death.

MASSINISSA
O Gelosso!
For thee full eyes—

SCIPIO
No passion for the rest?

MASSINISSA

O Scipio,
My grief for him may be expressed by tears,
But for the rest, silence, and secret anguish
Shall waste—shall waste! Scipio, he that can weep,
Grieves not, like me, private deep inward drops
Of blood. My heart! for god's right give me leave
To be a short time man.

SCIPIO

Stay, prince.

MASSINISSA

I cease;
Forgive if I forget thy presence. Scipio,
Thy face makes Massinissa more than man,
And here before your steady power a vow
As firm as fate I make: when I desist
To be commanded by thy virtue, Scipio,
Or fall from friend of Rome, revenging gods
Afflict me with your torture. I have given
Of passion and of faith, my heart.

SCIPIO

To counsel then;
Grief fits weak hearts, revenging virtue men.
Thus I think fit, before that Syphax know
How deeply Carthage sinks, let's beat swift march
Up even to Cirta, and whilst Syphax snores
With his, late thine—

MASSINISSA

With mine! no, Scipio;
Libya hath poison, asps, knives, and too much earth
To make one grave. With mine! Not; she can die.
Scipio, with mine! Jove, say it, thou dost lie.

SCIPIO

Temperance be Scipio's honour.

LÆLIUS

Cease your strife,
She is a woman.

MASSINISSA

But she is my wife.

LÆLIUS

And yet she is no god.

MASSINISSA
And yet she's more:
I do not praise gods' goodness, but adore;
Gods cannot fall, and for their constant goodness
(Which is necessited) they have a crown
Of never-ending pleasures; but faint man
(Framed to have his weakness made the heavens' glory),
If he with steady virtue holds all siege
That power, that speech, that pleasure, that full sweets,
A world of greatness can assail him with,
Having no pay but self-wept misery,
A beggar's treasure-heap,—that man I'll praise
Above the gods.

SCIPIO
The Libyan speaks bold sense.

MASSINISSA
By that by which all is, proportion,
I speak with thought.

SCIPIO
No more.

MASSINISSA
Forgive my admiration:
You touch'd a string to which my sense was quick.
Can you but think? Do, do; my grief—my grief—
Would make a saint blaspheme! Give some relief;
As thou art Scipio, forgive that I forget
I am a soldier. Such woes Jove's ribs would burst:
Few speak less ill that feel so much of worst.—
My ear attends.

SCIPIO
Before then Syphax join,
With new-strength'd Carthage, or can once unwind
His tangled sense from out so wild amaze,
Fall we like sudden lightning 'fore his eyes:
Boldness and speed are all of victories.

MASSINISSA
Scipio, let Massinissa clip thy knees!
May once these eyes view Syphax? shall this arm
Once make him feel his sin? O ye gods!
My cause, my cause! Justice is so huge odds,

That he who with it fears, heaven must renounce
In his creation.

SCIPIO
Beat then a close quick march!
Before the morn shall shake cold dews through skies,
Syphax shall tremble at Rome's thick alarms.

MASSINISSA
Ye powers, I challenge conquest to just arms.

[With a full flourish of cornets, they depart.

ACT IV

SCENE I

Near Cirta.

Enter **SOPHONISBA** and **ZANTHIA**, as out of a cave's mouth.

SOPHONISBA
Where are we, Zanthia?

ZANTHIA
Vangue said the cave
Opened in Belos' forest.

SOPHONISBA
Lord, how sweet
I scent the air! The huge long vault's close vein,
What damps it breath'd! In Belos' forest, say'st?
Be valiant, Zanthia; how far's Utica
From these most heavy shades?

ZANTHIA
Ten easy leagues.

SOPHONISBA
There's Massinissa: my true Zanthia,
Shall's venture nobly to escape, and touch
My lord's just arms? Love's wings so nimbly heave
The body up, that, as our toes shall trip
Over the tender and obedient grass,
Scarce any drop of dew is dash'd to ground.
And see the willing shade of friendly night

Makes safe our instant haste! Boldness and speed
Make actions most impossible succeed.

ZANTHIA
But, madam, know the forest hath no way
But one to pass, the which holds strictest guard.

SOPHONISBA
Do not betray me, Zanthia.

ZANTHIA
I, madam?

SOPHONISBA
No,
I not mistrust thee, yet—but—

ZANTHIA
Here you may
Delay your time.

SOPHONISBA
Ay, Zanthia, delay,
By which we may yet hope—yet hope—alas!
How all benumb'd's my sense! Chance hath so often struck
I scarce can feel. I should now curse the gods,
Call on the furies, stamp the patient earth.
Cleave my stretch'd cheeks with sound, speak from all sense,
But loud and full of players' eloquence.
No, no; what shall we eat?

ZANTHIA
Madam, I'll search
For some ripe nuts which autumn hath shook down
From the unleaved hazel, then some cooler air
Shall lead me to a spring. Or I will try
The courteous pale of some poor foresters
For milk.

SOPHONISBA
Do, Zanthia. O happiness

[Exit **ZANTHIA**.

Of those that know not pride or lust of city!
There's no man bless'd but those that most men pity.
O fortunate poor maids, that are not forced
To wed for state, nor are for state divorced!

Whom policy of kingdoms doth not marry,
But pure affection makes to love or vary;
You feel no love which you dare not to show,
Nor show a love which doth not truly grow!
O you are surely blessèd of the sky!
You live, that know not death before you die.

[Through the vaut's mouth, in his nightgown, torch in his hand, **SYPHAX** enters just behind
SOPHONISBA.

You are—

SYPHAX
In Syphax' arms. Thing of false lip,
What god shall now release thee?

SOPHONISBA
Art a man?

SYPHAX
Thy limbs shall feel. Despite thy virtue, know
I'll thread thy richest pearl. This forest's deaf
As is my lust. Night and the god of silence
Swells my full pleasures; no more shalt thou delude
My easy credence. Virgin of fair brow,
Well-featured creature, and our utmost wonder,
Queen of our youthful bed, be proud.

[**SYPHAX** setteth away his light, and prepareth to embrace **SOPHONISBA**.

I'll use thee.

[**SOPHONISBA** snatcheth out her knife.

SOPHONISBA
Look thee—view this—show but one strain of force,
Bow but to seize this arm, and by myself,
Or more, by Massinissa, this good steel
Shall set my soul on wing. Thus, form'd gods, see,
And, men with gods' worth, envy nought but me!

SYPHAX
Do, strike thy breast; know, being dead, I'll use,
With highest lust of sense, thy senseless flesh,
And even then thy vexèd soul shall see,
Without resistance, thy trunk prostitute
Unto our appetite.

SOPHONISBA

I shame to make thee know
How vile thou speakest; corruption then as much
As thou shalt do; but frame unto thy lusts
Imagination's utmost sin: Syphax,
I speak all frightless, know I live or die
To Massinissa; nor the force of fate
Shall make me leave his love, or slake thy hate.
I will speak no more.

SYPHAX

Thou hast amazed us: woman's forcèd use,
Like unripe fruits, no sooner got but waste;
They have proportion, colour, but no taste.—
[Aside]
Think, Syphax.—Sophonisba, rest thine own.
Our guard!

[Enter a **GUARD**.

Creature of most astonishing virtue,
If with fair usage, love, and passionate courtings,
We may obtain the heaven of thy bed,
We cease no suit; from other force be free:
We dote not on thy body, but love thee.

SOPHONISBA

Wilt thou keep faith?

SYPHAX

By thee, and by that power
By which thou art thus glorious, trust my vow.
Our guard convey the royal'st excellence
That ever was call'd woman to our palace:
Observe her with strict care.

SOPHONISBA

Dread Syphax, speak!
As thou art worthy, is not Zanthia false?

SYPHAX

To thee she is.

SOPHONISBA

As thou art then thyself,
Let her not be.

SYPHAX

She is not!

[The **GUARD** seizeth **ZANTHIA**.

ZANTHIA
Thus most speed:
When two foes are grown friends, partakers bleed.

SYPHAX
When plants must flourish, their manure must rot.

SOPHONISBA
Syphax, be recompensed, I hate thee not.

[Exeunt **SOPHONISBA**, **ZANTHIA**, and **GUARD**.

SYPHAX
A wasting flame feeds on my amorous blood,
Which we must cool, or die. What way all power,
All speech, full opportunity, can make,
We have made fruitless trial. Infernal Jove,
You resolute angels that delight in flames,
To you, all-wonder-working spirits, I fly!
Since heaven helps not, deepest hell we'll try
Here in this desert, the great soul of charms,
Dreadful Erictho lives, whose dismal brow
Contemns all roofs or civil coverture.
Forsaken graves and tombs, the ghosts forced out,
She joys to inhabit.
A loathsome yellow leanness spreads her face,
A heavy hell-like paleness loads her cheeks,
Unknown to a clear heaven; but if dark winds
Or thick black clouds drive back the blinded stars,
When her deep magic makes forced heaven quake
And thunder spite of Jove,—Erictho then
From naked graves stalks out, heaves proud her head
With long unkemb'd hair loaden, and strives to snatch
The night's quick sulphur; then she bursts up tombs,
From half-rot sear-cloths then she scrapes dry gums
For her black rites; but when she finds a corpse
But newly graved, whose entrails are not turn'd
To slimy filth, with greedy havock then
She makes fierce spoil, and swells with wicked triumph
To bury her lean knuckles in his eyes;
Then doth she gnaw the pale and o'ergrown nails
From his dry hand; but if she find some life
Yet lurking close, she bites his gelid lips,
And, sticking her black tongue in his dry throat,

She breathes dire murmurs, which enforce him bear
Her baneful secrets to the spirits of horror.
To her first sound the gods yield any harm,
As trembling once to hear a second charm:
She is—

[Infernal music plays softly whilst **ERICTHO** enters, and, when she speaks, ceaseth.

ERICTHO
Here, Syphax, here; quake not, for know
I know thy thoughts: thou wouldst entreat our power
Nice Sophonisba's passion to enforce
To thy affection, be all full of Jove.
'Tis done, 'tis done; to us heaven, earth, sea, air,
And Fate itself obeys; the beasts of death,
And all the terrors angry gods invented
(T'afflict the ignorance of patient man),
Tremble at us; the roll'd-up snake uncurls
His twisted knots at our affrighting voice.
Are we incensed? the king of flames grows pale,
Lest he be chok'd with black and earthy fumes,
Which our charms raise. Be joy'd, make proud thy lust:
I do not pray you, gods; my breath's, "You must."

SYPHAX
Deep knowing spirit, mother of all high
Mysterious science, what may Syphax yield
Worthy thy art, by which my soul's thus eased?
The gods first made me live, but thou live pleased.

ERICTHO
Know then, our love, hard by the reverent ruins
Of a once glorious temple rear'd to Jove,
Whose very rubbish (like the pitied fall
Of virtue most unfortunate) yet bears
A deathless majesty, though now quite rased,
Hurl'd down by wrath and lust of impious kings,
So that, where holy flamens wont to sing
Sweet hymns to heaven, there the daw and crow,
The ill-voiced raven, and still-chattering pie,
Send out ungrateful sounds and loathsome filth;
Where statues and Jove's acts were vively limn'd
Boys with black coals draw the veil'd parts of nature,
And lecherous actions of imagin'd lust;
Where tombs and beauteous urns of well-dead men
Stood in assurèd rest, the shepherd now
Unloads his belly, corruption most abhorr'd
Mingling itself with their renownèd ashes:

Ourself quakes at it!
There once a charnel-house, now a vast cave,
Over whose brow a pale and untrod grove
Throws out her heavy shade, the mouth thick arms
Of darksome yew (sun-proof) for ever choke;
Within rests barren darkness; fruitless drought
Pines in eternal night; the steam of hell
Yields not so lazy air: there, that's my cell;
From thence a charm, which Jove dare not hear twice,
Shall force her to thy bed. But, Syphax, know,
Love is the highest rebel to our art:
Therefore I charge thee, by the fear of all
Which thou know'st dreadful, or more, by ourself,
As with swift haste she passeth to thy bed,
And easy to thy wishes yields, speak not one word,
Nor dare, as thou dost fear thy loss of joys,
T'admit one light, one light.

SYPHAX
As to my fate
I yield my guidance.

ERICTHO
Then, when I shall force
The air to music, and the shades of night
To form sweet sounds, make proud thy raised delight:
Meantime, behold, I go a charm to rear,
Whose potent sound will force ourself to fear.

SYPHAX
Whither is Syphax heaved? at length shall's joy
Hopes more desired than heaven? Sweet labouring earth,
Let heaven be unform'd with mighty charms;
Let Sophonisba only fill these arms,
Jove we'll not envy thee. Blood's appetite
Is Syphax' god; my wisdom is my sense,
Without a man I hold no excellence.
Give me long breath, young beds, and sickness' ease;
For we hold firm, that's lawful which doth please.

[Infernal music, softly.

SYPHAX
Hark! hark! now rise infernal tones,
The deep-fetch'd groans
Of labouring spirits that attend
Erictho.

A VOICE [Within]
Erictho!

SYPHAX
Now crack the trembling earth, and send
Shrieks that portend
Affrightment to the gods which hear
Erictho.

A VOICE [Within]
Erictho!

[A treble viol, a base lute, &c., play softly within the canopy.

Hark! hark! now softer melody strikes mute
Disquiet Nature. O thou power of sound,
How thou dost melt me! Hark! now even heaven
Gives up his soul amongst us. Now's the time
When greedy expectation strains mine eyes
For their loved object; now Erictho will'd
Prepare my appetite for love's strict gripes.
O you dear founts of pleasure, blood, and beauty,
Raise active Venus worth fruition
Of such provoking sweetness. Hark, she comes!
A short song to soft music above.
Now nuptial hymns enforcèd spirits sing.
Hark, Syphax, hark! Now hell and heaven rings.

CANTANT.

With music spite of Phœbus. Peace! She comes!

[Enter **ERICTHO** in the shape of **SOPHONISBA**, her face veiled, and hasteth in the bed of Syphax.

Fury of blood's impatient! Erictho,
'Bove thunder sit: to thee, egregious soul,
Let all flesh bend. Sophonisba, thy flame
But equal mine, and we'll joy such delight,
That gods shall not admire, but even spite!

[**SYPHAX** hasteneth within the canopy, as to Sophonisba's bed.

ACT V

SCENE I

Bed-chamber in the palace of Syphax.

SYPHAX draws the curtains, and discovers **ERICTHO** lying with him.

ERICTHO
Ha! ha! ha!

SYPHAX
Light, light!

ERICTHO
Ha! ha!

SYPHAX
Thou rotten scum of hell!
O my abhorrèd heat! O loath'd delusion!

[They leap out of the bed; **SYPHAX** takes him to his sword.

ERICTHO
Why! fool of kings, could thy weak soul imagine
That 'tis within the grasp of heaven or hell
To enforce love? Why, know love dotes the fates,
Jove groans beneath his weight: mere ignorant thing,
Know we, Erictho, with a thirsty womb,
Have coveted full threescore suns for blood of kings.
We that can make enraged Neptune toss
His huge curl'd locks without one breath of wind;
We that can make heaven slide from Atlas' shoulder;
We, in the pride and height of covetous lust,
Have wish'd with woman's greediness to fill
Our longing arms with Syphax' well-strung limbs:
And dost thou think, if philters or hell-charms
Could have enforced thy use, we would have deigned
Brain sleights? No, no. Now are we full
Of our dear wishes. Thy proud heat, well wasted,
Hath made our limbs grow young! Our love, farewell!
Know he that would force love, thus seeks his hell.

[**ERICTHO** slips into the ground, as **SYPHAX** offers his sword to her.

SYPHAX
Can we yet breathe? Is any plagued like me?
Are we—let's think—O now contempt, my hate
To thee, thy thunder, sulphur, and scorn'd name!
He whose life's loath'd, and he who breathes to curse
His very being, let him thus with me

[**SYPHAX** kneels at the altar.

Fall 'fore an altar, sacred to black powers,
And thus dare heavens! O thou whose blasting flames
Hurl barren droughts upon the patient earth,
And thou, gay god of riddles and strange tales,
Hot-brainèd Phœbus, all add if you can
Something unto my misery! if aught
Of plagues lurk in your deep-trench'd brows,
Which yet I know not,—let them fall like bolts,
Which wrathful Jove drives strong into my bosom!
If any chance of war, or news ill-voiced,
Mischief unthought of lurk, come, give't us all,
Heap curse on curse, we can no lower fall!

[Out of the altar the ghost of **ASDRUBAL** ariseth.

ASDRUBAL
Lower—lower!

SYPHAX
What damn'd air is form'd
Into that shape? Speak, speak, we cannot quake!
Our flesh knows not ignoble tremblings. Speak!
We dare thy terror. Methinks hell and fate
Should dread a soul with woes made desperate.

ASDRUBAL
Know me the spirit of great Asdrubal,
Father to Sophonisba, whose bad heart
Made justly most unfortunate; for know,
I turn'd unfaithful, after that the field
Chanced to our loss, when of thy men there fell
Six thousand souls, next fight of Libyans ten.
After which loss we unto Carthage flying,
Th' enragèd people cried their army fell
Through my base treason. Straight my revengeful Furies
Makes them pursue me; I with resolute haste
Made to the grave of all our ancestors,
Where poisoned, hoped my bones should have long rest:
But see, the violent multitude arrives,
Tear down our monument, and me now dead
Deny a grave; hurl us among the rocks
To staunch beasts' hunger; therefore thus ungraved
I seek slow rest. Now dost thou know more woes,
And more must feel. Mortals, O fear to slight
Your gods and vows. Jove's arm is of dread might.

SYPHAX
Yet speak: shall I o'ercome approaching foes?

ASDRUBAL
Spirits of wrath know nothing but their woes.

[Exit.

[Enter **NUNTIUS**.

NUNTIUS
My liege, my liege,
The scouts of Cirta bring intelligence
Of sudden danger; full ten thousand horse,
Fresh and well-rid, strong Massinissa leads,
As wings to Roman legions that march swift,
Led by that man of conquest, Scipio.

SYPHAX
Scipio?

NUNTIUS
Direct to Cirta.

[A march far off is heard.

Hark! their march is heard even to the city.

SYPHAX
Help! our guard! my arms!
Bid all our leaders march! beat thick alarms!
I have seen things which thou wouldst quake to hear.
Boldness and strength! the shame of slaves be fear.
Up, heart, hold sword! though waves roll thee on shelf,
Though fortune leave thee, leave not thou thyself!

[Exit, arming.

SCENE II

Neighbourhood of Cirta.

Enter **TWO PAGES**, with targets and javelins; **LÆLIUS** and **JUGURTH**, with halberds; **SCIPIO** and **MASSINISSA** armed; cornets sounding a march.

SCIPIO

Stand!

MASSINISSA
Give the word—Stand!

SCIPIO
Part the file!

MASSINISSA
Give way!
Scipio, by thy great name, but greater virtue,—
By our eternal love, give me the chance
Of this day's battle! Let not thy envied fame
Vouchsafe t'oppose the Roman legions
Against one weakened Prince of Libya.
This quarrel's mine—mine be the stroke of fight!
Let us and Syphax hurl out well-forced darts
Each unto other's breast. O (what should I say?)
Thou beyond epithet, thou whom proud lords of fortune
May even envy,—alas! my joy's so vast
Makes me seem lost,—let us thunder and lightning
Strike from our brave arms! Look, look, seize that hill!
Hark! he comes near. From thence discern us strike
Fire worth Jove; mount up, and not repute
Me very proud, though wondrous resolute.
My cause, my cause is my bold heart'ning odds,
That sevenfold shield; just arms should fright the gods.

SCIPIO
Thy words are full of honour; take thy fate.

MASSINISSA
Which we do scorn to fear, to Scipio state
Worthy his heart. Now let the forcèd brass
Sound on!

[Cornets sound a march. **SCIPIO** leads his train up to the mount.

Jugurth, clasp sure our casque,
Arm us with care; and Jugurth, if I fall
Through this day's malice or our fathers' sins,
If it in thy sword lie, break up my breast,
And save my heart that never fell nor sued
To aught but Jove and Sophonisba. Sound,
Stern heart'ners unto wounds and blood—sound loud,
For we have namèd Sophonisba!

[Cornets, a flourish.

So!

[Cornets, a march far off.

Hark, hark, he comes! stand blood! Now multiply
Force more than fury. Sound high, sound high, we strike
For Sophonisba!

[Enter **SYPHAX**, arm'd, his **PAGES** with shields and darts before; cornets sounding marches.

SYPHAX
For Sophonisba!

MASSINISSA
Syphax!

SYPHAX
Massinissa!

MASSINISSA
Betwixt us two,
Let single fight try all.

SYPHAX
Well urged.

MASSINISSA
Well granted.
Of you, my stars, as I am worthy you,
I implore aid; and O, if angels wait
Upon good hearts, my genius be as strong
As I am just.

SYPHAX
Kings' glory is their wrong.
He that may only do just acts 's a slave.
My god's my arm; my life my heaven; my grave
To me all end.

MASSINISSA
Give day, gods,—life, not death,—
To him that only fears blaspheming breath.
For Sophonisba!

SYPHAX
For Sophonisba!

[Cornets sound a charge. **MASSINISSA** and **SYPHAX** combat. **SYPHAX** falls. **MASSINISSA** unclasps Syphax' casque, and is about to kill him when **SYPHAX** speaks.

SYPHAX
Unto thy fortune, not to thee, we yield.

MASSINISSA
Lives Sophonisba yet unstain'd, speak just—
Yet ours unforced?

SYPHAX
Let my heart fall more low
Than is my body, if only to thy glory
She lives not yet all thine.

MASSINISSA
Rise, rise! Cease strife!
Hear a most deep revenge—from us take life!

[Cornets sound a march. **SCIPIO** and **LÆLIUS** enter. **SCIPIO** passeth to his throne. **MASSINISSA** presents **SYPHAX** to Scipio's feet, cornets sounding a flourish.

To you all power of strength; and next to thee,
Thou spirit of triumph, born for victory,
I heave these hands. March we to Cirta straight,
My Sophonisba with swift haste to win,
In honour and in love all mean is sin.

[Exeunt **MASSINISSA** and **JUGURTH**.

SCIPIO
As we are Rome's great general, thus we press
Thy captive neck. But as still Scipio,
And sensible of just humanity,
We weep thy bondage. Speak, thou ill-chanced man,
What spirit took thee when thou wert our friend
(Thy right hand given both to gods and us,
With such most passionate vows and solemn faith),
Thou fled'st with such most foul disloyalty
To now weak Carthage? strengthening their bad arms,
Who lately scorn'd thee with all loath'd abuse,
Who never entertain for love but use?

SYPHAX
Scipio, my fortune is captived, not I,
Therefore I'll speak bold truth; nor once mistrust
What I shall say, for now, being wholly yours,
I must not feign. Sophonisba, 'twas she,

'Twas Sophonisba that solicited
My forced revolt; 'twas her resistless suit,
Her love to her dear Carthage, 'ticed me break
All faith with men; 'twas she made Syphax false;
She that loves Carthage with such violence,
And hath such moving graces to allure,
That she will turn a man that once hath sworn
Himself on's father's bones her Carthage foe,
To be that city's champion and high friend.
Her hymeneal torch burnt down my house;
Then was I captived, when her wanton arms
Threw moving clasps about my neck. O charms,
Able to turn even Fate! But this, in my true grief,
Is some just joy, that my love-sotted foe
Shall seize that plague; that Massinissa's breast
Her hands shall arm, and that ere long you'll try
She can force him your foe as well as I.

SCIPIO
Lælius, Lælius, take a choice troop of horse,
And spur to Cirta. To Massinissa thus:
Syphax' palace, crown's spoil, city's sack,
Be free to him. But if our new-leagued friend
Possess that woman of so moving art,
Charge him with no less weight than his dear vow,
Our love, all faith, that he resign her thee;
As he shall answer Rome, will him give up
A Roman prisoner to the Senate's doom:
She is a Carthaginian. Now our law's—
Wise men prevent not actions, but ever cause.

SYPHAX
Good Malice, so, as liberty so dear,
Prove my revenge. What I cannot possess
Another shall not—that's some happiness.

SCENE III

Cirta.

Cornets afar off sounding a charge. A **SOLDIER** wounded at one door. Enter at the other **SOPHONISBA**, **TWO PAGES** before her with lights, **TWO WOMEN** bearing up her train.

SOLDIER
Princess, O fly! Syphax hath lost the day,
And captived lies. The Roman legions

Have seiz'd the town, and with inveterate hate
Make slaves, or murder all. Fire and steel,
Fury and night, hold all. Fair Queen, O fly!
We bleed for Carthage, all for Carthage die!

[Exit.

[Cornets sounding a march. Enter **PAGES** with javelins and targets. **MASSINISSA** and **JUGURTH**;
Massinissa's beaver shut.

MASSINISSA
March to the palace.

SOPHONISBA
Whate'er man thou art,
Of Libya thy fair arms speak, give heart
To amazed weakness; hear her, that for long time
Hath seen no wishèd light. Sophonisba,
A name for misery much known, 'tis she
Entreats of thy graced sword this only boon:—
Let me not kneel to Rome; for though no cause
Of mine deserves their hate, though Massinissa
Be ours to heart, yet Roman generals
Make proud their triumphs with whatever captives.
O 'tis a nation which from soul I fear,
As one well knowing the much-grounded hate
They bear to Asdrubal and Carthage blood;
Therefore with tears that wash thy feet, with hands
Unused to beg, I clasp thy manly knees:
O save me from their fetters and contempt,
Their proud insults and more than insolence!
Or, if it rest not in thy grace of breath
To grant such freedom, give me long-wish'd death;
For 'tis not now loath'd life that we do crave,—
Only an unshamed death and silent grave,
We will now deign to bend for.

MASSINISSA
Rarity!

[**MASSINISSA** disarms his head.

By thee and this right hand, thou shalt live free!

SOPHONISBA
We cannot now be wretched.

MASSINISSA

Stay the sword!
Let slaughter cease; sounds soft as Leda's breast

[Soft music.

Slide through all ears. This night be love's high feast.

SOPHONISBA
O'erwhelm me not with sweets; let me not drink
Till my breast burst, O Jove, thy nectar-skink.

[She sinks into **MASSINISSA'S** arms.

MASSINISSA
She is o'ercome with joy!

SOPHONISBA
Help—help to bar
Some happiness, ye powers! I have joy to spare,
Enough to make a god! O Massinissa!

MASSINISSA
Peace!
A silent thinking makes full joys increase!

[Enter **LÆLIUS**.

LÆLIUS
Massinissa!

MASSINISSA
Lælius!

LÆLIUS
Thine ear.

MASSINISSA
Stand off.

LÆLIUS
From Scipio thus: by thy late vow of faith,
And mutual league of endless amity,
As thou respects his virtue, or Rome's force,
Deliver Sophonisba to our hand.

MASSINISSA
Sophonisba?

LÆLIUS
Sophonisba.

SOPHONISBA
My lord
Looks pale, and from his half-burst eyes a flame
Of deep disquiet breaks. The gods turn false
My sad presage!

MASSINISSA
Sophonisba?

LÆLIUS
Even she.

MASSINISSA
She kill'd not Scipio's father, nor his uncle,
Great Cneius.

LÆLIUS
Carthage did!

MASSINISSA
To her what's Carthage?

LÆLIUS
Know 'twas her father Asdrubal strook off
His father's head. Give place to faith and fate!

MASSINISSA
'Tis cross to honour.

LÆLIUS
But 'tis just to state.
So speaketh Scipio. Do not thou detain
A Roman prisoner, due to this great triumph,
As thou shalt answer Rome and him.

MASSINISSA
Lælius,
We now are in Rome's power. Lælius,
View Massinissa do a loathèd act,
Most sinking from that state his heart did keep.
Look, Lælius, look, see Massinissa weep!
Know I have made a vow, more dear to me
Than my soul's endless being, she shall rest
Free from Rome's bondage!

LÆLIUS
But dost thou forget
Thy vow, yet fresh, thus breath'd: When I desist
To be commanded by thy virtue, Scipio,
Or fall from friend of Rome, revenging gods,
Afflict me with your torture!

MASSINISSA
Lælius, enough.

LÆLIUS
Salute the Roman, tell him we will act
What shall amaze him.

LÆLIUS
Wilt thou yield her then?

MASSINISSA
She shall arrive there straight.

LÆLIUS
Best fate of men
To thee.

MASSINISSA
And Scipio.—Have I lived, O heavens,

[Exit **LÆLIUS** with **PAGES**.

To be enforcedly perfidious?

SOPHONISBA
What unjust grief afflicts my worthy lord?

MASSINISSA
Thank me, ye gods, with much beholdingness;
For mark, I do not curse you.

SOPHONISBA
Tell me, sweet,
The cause of thy much anguish.

MASSINISSA
Ha, the cause?
Let's see: wreathe back thine arms, bend down thy neck,
Practise base prayers, make fit thyself for bondage.

SOPHONISBA

Bondage!

MASSINISSA
Bondage—Roman bondage!

SOPHONISBA
No, no!

MASSINISSA
How then have I vow'd well to Scipio?

SOPHONISBA
How then to Sophonisba?

MASSINISSA
Right, which way?
Run mad!—impossible!—distraction!

SOPHONISBA
Dear lord, thy patience; let it maze all power,
And list to her in whose sole heart it rests
To keep thy faith upright.

MASSINISSA
Wilt thou be slaved?

SOPHONISBA
No, free.

MASSINISSA
How then keep I my faith?

SOPHONISBA
My death
Gives help to all. From Rome so rest we free;
So brought to Scipio, faith is kept in thee.

MASSINISSA
Thou darest not die—some wine!—thou darest not die!

[Enter a **PAGE** with a bowl of wine.

SOPHONISBA
How near was I unto the curse of man. Joy!
How like was I yet once to have been glad!
He that ne'er laugh'd may with a constant face
Contemn Jove's frown: happiness makes us base.

[She takes the bowl, into which **MASSINISSA** puts poison.

Behold me, Massinissa, like thyself,
A king and soldier; and I prithee keep
My last command.

MASSINISSA
Speak, sweet.

SOPHONISBA
Dear, do not weep.
And now with undismay'd resolve behold,
To save you—you (for honour and just faith
Are most true gods, which we should much adore),
With even disdainful vigour I give up
An abhorr'd life. You have been good to me,

[She drinks.

And I do thank thee, heaven! O my stars,
I bless your goodness, that with breast unstain'd,
Faith pure, a virgin wife, tried to my glory,
I die, of female faith the long-lived story;
Secure from bondage and all servile harms,
But more—most happy in my husband's arms.

[She sinks.

JUGURTH
Massinissa, Massinissa!

MASSINISSA
Covetous,
Fame-greedy lady, could no scope of glory,
No reasonable proportion of goodness,
Fill thy great breast, but thou must prove immense
Incomprehence in virtue! What, wouldst thou
Not only be admired, but even adored?
O glory ripe for heaven! Sirs, help, help, help!
Let us to Scipio with what speed you can;
For piety make haste, whilst yet we are man.

[Exeunt, bearing **SOPHONISBA** in a chair.

SCENE IV

Neighbourhood of Cirta.

Cornets a march. Enter **SCIPIO** in full state, triumphal ornaments carried before him, and **SYPHAX** bound; at the other door, **LÆLIUS**.

SCIPIO
What answers Massinissa? Will he send
That Sophonisba of so moving tongue?

LÆLIUS
Full of dismay'd unsteadiness he stood,
His right hand lock'd in hers, which hand he gave
As pledge for Rome she ever should live free.
But when I enter'd and well urged this vow
And thy command, his great heart sunk with shame,
His eyes lost spirit, and his heat of life
Sank from his face, as one that stood benumb'd,
All mazed, t'effect impossibilities;
For either unto her or Scipio
He must break vow. Long time he toss'd his thoughts;
And as you see a snow-ball being roll'd,
At first a handful, yet, long bowl'd about,
Insensibly acquires a mighty globe,—
So his cold grief through agitation grows,
And more he thinks, the more of grief he knows.
At last he seem'd to yield her.

SYPHAX
Mark, Scipio!
Trust him that breaks a vow?

SCIPIO
How then trust thee?

SYPHAX
O, misdoubt him not, when he's thy slave like me.

[Enter **MASSINISSA**, all in black.

MASSINISSA
Scipio!

SCIPIO
Massinissa!

MASSINISSA
General!

SCIPIO
King!

MASSINISSA
Lives there no mercy for one soul of Carthage,
But must see baseness?

SCIPIO
Wouldst thou joy thy peace,
Deliver Sophonisba straight and cease;
Do not grasp that which is too hot to hold.
We grace thy grief, and hold it with soft sense;
Enjoy good courage, but 'void insolence.
I tell thee Rome and Scipio deign to bear
So low a breast as for her say—we fear.

MASSINISSA
Do not, do not; let not the fright of nations
Know so vile terms. She rests at thy dispose.

SYPHAX
To my soul's joy. Shall Sophonisba then
With me go bound, and wait on Scipio's wheel?
When th' whole world's giddy, one man cannot reel.

MASSINISSA
Starve thy lean hopes; and, Romans, now behold
A sight would sad the gods, make Phœbus cold.

[Organ and recorders play to a single voice. Enter in the meantime the mournful solemnity of
MASSINISSA'S presenting **SOPHONISBA'S** body.

Look, Scipio, see what hard shift we make
To keep our vows. Here, take, I yield her thee;
And Sophonisba, I keep vow, thou'rt still free.

SYPHAX
Burst, my vex'd heart: the torture that most racks
An enemy is his foe's royal acts.

SCIPIO
The glory of thy virtue live for ever;
Brave hearts may be obscured, but extinct never.

[**SCIPIO** adorns **MASSINISSA**.

Take from the general of Rome this crown,
This robe of triumph, and this conquest's wreath,

This sceptre and this hand; for ever breathe
Rome's very minion. Live worth thy fame,
As far from faintings as from now base name.

MASSINISSA
Thou whom, like sparkling steel, the strokes of chance
Made hard and firm, and, like wild-fire turn'd,
The more cold fate, the more thy virtue burn'd,
And in whole seas of miseries didst flame;
On thee, loved creature of a deathless fame,

[**MASSINISSA** adorns **SOPHONISBA**.

Rest all my honour! O thou for whom I drink
So deep of grief, that he must only think,
Not dare to speak, that would express my woe;
Small rivers murmur, deep gulfs silent flow.
My grief is here, not here: heave gently then,
Women's right wonder, and just shame of men.

[Exeunt **ALL** but **MASSINISSA**.

[Cornets a short flourish.

EPILOGUS

MASSINISSA
And now
With lighter passion, though with most just fear,
I change my person, and do hither bear
Another's voice, who with a phrase as weak
As his deserts, now will'd me (thus form'd) speak:
If words well sensed, best suiting subject grave,
Noble true story, may once boldly crave
Acceptance gracious; if he whose fires
Envy not others, nor himself admires;
If scenes exempt from ribaldry or rage
Of taxings indiscreet, may please the stage;—
If such may hope applause, he not commands,
Yet craves as due the justice of your hands.
But freely he protests, howe'er it is—
Or well, or ill, or much, not much amiss—
With constant modesty he does submit
To all, save those that have more tongue than wit.

John Marston was born to John and Maria Marston née Guarsi, and baptised on October 7th, 1576 at Wardington, Oxfordshire. His father was an eminent lawyer of the Middle Temple who first practiced in London and then became the counsel to Coventry and later its steward.

Marston entered Brasenose College, Oxford in 1592 and earned his BA in 1594. By 1595, he was in London, living in the Middle Temple. His interests were in poetry and play writing, although his father's will of 1599 hopes that he would not further pursue such vanities.

His brief career in literature began with a foray into the then fashionable genres of erotic epyllion and satire; erotic plays for boy actors to be performed before educated young men and members of the inns of court.

In 1598, he published 'The Metamorphosis of Pigmalion's Image and Certaine Satyres', a book of poetry in imitation of, on the one hand, Ovid, and, on the other, the Satires of Juvenal. He also published 'The Scourge of Villanie', in 1598. (these were issued under the pseudonym "W. Kinsayder.") The satire in these books is even more savage and misanthropic than the prevailing norm for other satirists of the era. Marston's style sometimes bends to the point of unintelligibility: he believed that satire should be rough and obscure. Marston seems to have been enraged by Joseph Hall's claim to be the first satirist in English; Hall comes in for some indirect retribution later in one or more of his satires. Some see William Shakespeare's Thersites and Iago, as well as the mad speeches of King Lear as influenced by 'The Scourge of Villanie'.

Marston had, however, arrived on the literary scene as the fad for verse satire was coming under pressure from the authority's censors. Both the Archbishop of Canterbury and the Bishop of London banned 'The Scourge of Villanie' had it publicly burned, along with copies of works by other satirists, on 4th June 1599.

In September 1599, John Marston began to work for the famed Philip Henslowe as a playwright. Marston proved a good match for the private stage where boy players performed racy dramas for an audience of city gallants and young members of the Inns of Court.

'Histriomastix' has been regarded as his first play; performed by either the Children of Paul's or the students of the Middle Temple in around 1599. Its performance kicked off an episode in literary history commonly known as the 'War of the Theatres'; the literary feud between Marston, Jonson and Dekker that took place between 1599 and 1602.

Around 1600, Marston wrote 'Jack Drum's Entertainment' and 'Antonio and Mellida', and in 1601 he wrote 'Antonio's Revenge', a sequel to the latter play; all three were performed by the company at Paul's. In 1601, he contributed poems to Robert Chester's 'Love's Martyr'. For Henslowe, he may have also collaborated with Dekker, Day, and Haughton on 'Lust's Dominion'.

By 1601, he was well known in London literary circles, particularly in his role as enemy to the equally brilliant and difficult Ben Jonson. Jonson, who reported that Marston had accused him of sexual profligacy, satirized Marston as Clove in 'Every Man Out of His Humour', as Crispinus in 'Poetaster', and as Hedon in 'Cynthia's Revels'. Jonson thought Marston a false poet, a vain, careless writer who plagiarised the works of others and whose works were marked by bizarre diction and ugly neologisms. For his part, Marston used Jonson as the complacent, arrogant critic Brabant Senior in 'Jack Drum's Entertainment' and as the envious, misanthropic playwright and satirist Lampatho Doria in 'What You Will'.

'The Return from Parnassus (II)', an anonymous and satirical play performed at St. John's College, Cambridge in 1601 and 1602, characterised Marston as a poet whose writings see him 'pissing against the world'.

Jonson states that at one point their 'War' boiled over into the physical when he had beaten Marston and taken his pistol. However, the two playwrights were reconciled; Marston wrote a prefatory poem for Jonson's 'Sejanus' in 1605 and dedicated 'The Malcontent' to him.

Beyond this episode Marston's career continued to gather both strength, assets and followers. In 1603, he became a shareholder in the Children of Blackfriars company, at that time known for steadily pushing the boundaries of personal satire, violence, and lewdness on stage. He wrote and produced two plays with the company. The first was 'The Malcontent' in 1603, his most famous play. This work was originally written for the children at Blackfriars and was later taken over by the Kings' Men at the Globe, with additions by John Webster. His second play for the Blackfriars children was 'The Dutch Courtesan', a satire on lust and hypocrisy, in 1604-5.

In 1605, he worked with George Chapman and Ben Jonson on 'Eastward Ho', a satire of popular taste and the vain imaginings of wealth to be found in the colony of Virginia. Chapman and Jonson were arrested for, according to Jonson, a few clauses that offended the Scots, but Marston escaped any imprisonment. Their detainment was brief, and the charges were dropped.

He married Mary Wilkes in 1605, the daughter of the Reverend William Wilkes, one of the chaplains to King James.

In 1606, Marston seems to have had mixed fortunes with the king. At times offending and at others pleasing. In 'Parasitaster, or, The Fawn', he satirized the king specifically. However, in the summer of that year, he put on a production of 'The Dutch Courtesan' for the King of Denmark's visit, with a Latin verse on King James that was presented by hand to the king. Finally, in 1607, he wrote 'The Entertainment at Ashby', a masque for the Earl of Huntingdon.

Marston took the theatre world by surprise when he gave up writing plays in 1609 at the age of thirty-three. He sold his shares in the company of Blackfriars. His departure from the literary scene may have been because of further offence he gave to the king. The king suspended performances at Blackfriars and had Marston imprisoned.

After release he moved into his father-in-law's house to study philosophy. In 1609, he became a reader at the Bodleian library at Oxford. On 24th September he was made a deacon and then a priest on 24th December 1609. In October 1616, Marston was assigned the living of Christchurch, Hampshire.

He died (accounts vary) on either the 24th or 25th June 1634 in London and was buried in the Middle Temple Church.

Tombs at that time were often inscribed with 'Memoriae Sacrum' ('Sacred to the memory') and then the occupants name and a brief account of their achievements. According to Anthony à Wood Marston's tomb stone read 'Oblivioni Sacrum' ('Sacred to Oblivion'), which was probably composed by Marston, and both self-abasing and witty in upturning the tradition.

Marston's reputation through the centuries has varied widely, like that of most of the minor Renaissance dramatists. Both 'The Malcontent' and 'The Dutch Courtesan' remained on stage in altered forms throughout the Restoration.

After the Restoration, Marston's works were largely reduced to literary history. The general resemblance of 'The Malcontent' to 'Hamlet' and Marston's role in the 'War of the Theatres' ensured that his plays would receive some scholarly attention, but they were not performed, nor widely read.

The Romantic movement in English literature unevenly resuscitated Marston's reputation. In his lectures, William Hazlitt praised Marston's genius for satire; however, if the romantic critics were willing to grant Marston's best work a place among the great accomplishments of the age, they remained aware of his inconsistency, what Swinburne would later call his 'uneven and irregular demesne'.

In the twentieth century, however, a few critics were willing to consider Marston as a writer who was very much in control of the world he created. T. S. Eliot saw that this 'irregular demesne' was a part of Marston's world and that "It is ... by giving us the sense of something behind, more real than any of the personages and their action, that Marston establishes himself among the writers of genius".

John Marston – A Concise Bibliography

Plays and production dates

Histriomastix (play), 1599
Antonio and Mellida, London, Paul's theater, 1599–1600.
Jack Drum's Entertainment, London, Paul's theater, 1599/1600.
Antonio's Revenge, London, Paul's theater, 1600.
What You Will, London, Paul's theater, 1601.
The Malcontent, London, Blackfriars Theatre, 1603–1604; Globe Theatre, 1604.
Parasitaster, or The Fawn, London, Blackfriars theater, 1604.
Eastward Ho, by Marston, George Chapman, and Ben Jonson, London, Blackfriars theater, 1604–1605.
The Dutch Courtesan, London, Blackfriars theater, 1605.
The Wonder of Women, or The Tragedy of Sophonisba, London, Blackfriars theater, 1606.
The Spectacle Presented to the Sacred Majesties of Great Britain, and Denmark as They Passed through London, London, 31 July 1606.
The Entertainment of the Dowager-Countess of Darby, Ashby-de-la-Zouch in Leicestershire, 1607.
The Insatiate Countess, by Marston and William Barksted, London, Whitefriars Theatre, c 1608.

Books

The Metamorphosis of Pigmalions Image. And Certaine Satyres.

The Scourge of Villanie. Three Bookes of Satyres (1598; revised and enlarged edition, 1599)
Jacke Drums Entertainment: Or, The Comedie of Pasquill and Katherine (1601)
Loves Martyr: or, Rosalins Complaint, by Marston, Ben Jonson, William Shakespeare, and George Chapman (1601)
The History of Antonio and Mellida (1602)
Antonios Revenge (1602)
The Malcontent (1604)
Eastward Hoe, by Marston, Chapman, and Jonson (1605)
The Dutch Courtezan (1605)
Parasitaster, or The Fawne (1606)
The Wonder of Women, or The Tragedie of Sophonisba (1606)
What You Will (1607)
Histrio-mastix: Or, The Player Whipt (1610)
The Insatiate Countesse, by Marston and William Barksted (1613)
The Workes of Mr. J. Marston (1633); republished as Tragedies and Comedies (1633)
Comedies, Tragi-comedies; & Tragedies, Nonce Collection (1652)
Lust's Dominion, or The Lascivious Queen (probably the same play as The Spanish Moor's Tragedy), by Marston, Thomas Dekker, John Day, and William Haughton (1657)

www.ingramcontent.com/pod-product-compliance
Lightning Source LLC
Chambersburg PA
CBHW021940040426
42448CB00008B/1163